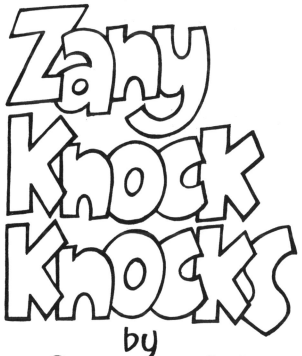

Zany Knock Knocks

by
Ronny M. Cole

Illustrated by
Rich Garramone

 Sterling Publishing Co., Inc. New York

To Adam and Arielle

Library of Congress Cataloging-in-Publication Data

Cole, Ronny M.
    Zany knock-knocks / Ronny M. Cole ; illustrated by Rich Garramone.
        p.   cm.
    Includes index.
    Summary: A collection of knock-knock jokes arranged alphabetically.
    ISBN 0-8069-8588-7
    1. Knock-knock jokes.   2. Wit and humor, Juvenile.   [1. Knock-knock
jokes.   2. Jokes.]   I. Garramone, Rich, ill.   II. Title.
PN6231.K55C65   1993
818′.5402—dc20   92-43068
                                                                                                                              CIP
                                                                                                                              AC

Cover design by Sanford Hoffman

20 19 18 17

Published in 1993 by Sterling Publishing Company, Inc.
387 Park Avenue South, New York, N.Y. 10016
Text © 1993 by Ronny M. Cole
Illustrations © 1993 by Rich Garramone
Distributed in Canada by Sterling Publishing
% Canadian Manda Group, P.O. Box 920, Station U
Toronto, Ontario, Canada M8Z 5P9
Distributed in Great Britain by Chrysalis Books
64 Brewery Road, London N7 9NT, England
Distributed in Australia by Capricorn Link (Australia) Pty.
P.O. Box 704, Windsor, NSW 2756 Australia

Sterling ISBN 0-8069-8589-5 Paper
ISBN 0-8069-8588-7 Trade

A

Knock-knock.
  Who's there?
Aaron.
  Aaron who?
Why Aaron you
opening the door?

Knock-knock.
  Who's there?
Abe.
  Abe who?
Abe out face!

Knock-knock.
  Who's there?
Abe Lincoln.
  Abe Lincoln who?
Abe Lincoln
(a blinkin') yellow
light means slow down!

Knock-knock.
  Who's there?
Abercrombie.
  Abercrombie who?
Abercrombie (have a crumby)
time at the party!

Knock-knock.
  Who's there?
Abyssinia.
  Abyssinia who?
Abyssinia at the mall!

Knock-knock.
  Who's there?
Acey Ducey.
  Acey Ducey who?
Acey your point,
Ducey mine?

Knock-knock.
  Who's there?
Adam.
  Adam who?
Adam my way—
I'm coming in!

Knock-knock.
  Who's there?
A La Mode.
  A La Mode who?
Remember the A La Mode (Alamo)!

Knock-knock.
  Who's there?
Aldous.
  Aldous who?
Aldous fuss over
little ol' me?

Knock-knock.
  Who's there?
Aldus.
  Aldus who?
Aldus talk
and no action!

Knock-knock.
  Who's there?
Alice.
  Alice who?
Alice fair in love and war!

Knock-knock.
  Who's there?
Alistair.
  Alistair who?
You uncover the pot, Alistair the soup!

  Knock-knock.
    Who's there?
  Altoona.
    Altoona who?
  Altoona piano—you play it!

    Knock-knock.
      Who's there?
    Brinckerhoff.
      Brinckerhoff who?
    You Brinckerhoff the soda—
    I'll bring the other half.

Knock-knock.
  Who's there?
Alma.
  Alma who?
The dog ate Alma
homework!

Knock-knock.
  Who's there?
Amana.
  Amana who?
Amana-eating tiger!

Knock-knock.
  Who's there?
Camellia.
  Camellia who?
Camellia little
closer.

Knock-knock.
  Who's there?
Meteor.
  Meteor who?
Prepare to Meteor (meet your) maker!

Knock-knock.
  Who's there?
Amahl.
  Amahl who?
Amahl tied up,
call me later!

Knock-knock.
  Who's there?
Amarillo.
  Amarillo who?
Amarillo nice guy.

Knock-knock.
  Who's there?
Amerigo.
  Amerigo who?
Amerigo-round.

  Knock-knock.
    Who's there?
  Vespucci.
    Vespucci who?
  How much is Vespucci (that poochie)
  in the window?

Knock-knock.
  Who's there?
Arcudi.
  Arcudi who?
Arcudi little dog
can do one trick.

Knock-knock.
  Who's there?
Annapolis.
  Annapolis who?
Annapolis day keeps the doctor away.

Knock-knock.
  Who's there?
Angela.
  Angela who?
Angela Mercy.

Knock-knock.
  Who's there?
Anita.
  Anita who?
Anita rest!

Knock-knock.
  Who's there?
Anna Mary.
  Anna Mary who?
"Anna Mary old
soul was he . . ."

Knock-knock.
  Who's there?
Antilles.
  Antilles who?
Antilles open the door,
I'm gonna sit here on your doorstep!

Knock-knock.
  Who's there?
Ariel.
  Ariel who?
You're Ariel pain in the neck!

  Knock-knock.
    Who's there?
  Cosmo.
    Cosmo who?
  You Cosmo trouble
  than you're worth!

Knock-knock.
  Who's there?
Amish.
  Amish who?
Amish you sho mush!!

Knock-knock.
  Who's there?
Armstrong.
  Armstrong who?
Armstrong as an ox—
and you have the brain
of one.

  Knock-knock.
    Who's there?
  Arsenio Hall.
    Arsenio Hall who?
Arsenio Hall (I've seen you all) over town!

9

Knock-knock.
  Who's there?
Artichoke.
  Artichoke who?
Artichoke on a
chicken bone.

Knock-knock.
  Who's there?
Artie Fish.
  Artie Fish who?
Artie Fish-el
intelligence!

Knock-knock.
  Who's there?
Aruba.
  Aruba who?
Aruba (are you the) one in charge?

Knock-knock.
  Who's there?
Ashley.
  Ashley who?
Ashley, I'm not sure . . .

Knock-knock.
  Who's there?
Asbestos.
  Asbestos who?
I'm doing Asbestos I can!

Knock-knock.
  Who's there?
Astoria.
  Astoria who?
I've got Astoria wouldn't believe!

  Knock-knock.
    Who's there?
  Boris.
    Boris who?
  Go ahead, Boris with another story!

Knock-knock.
  Who's there?
Attila.
  Attila who?
Attila we meet again!

Knock-knock.
  Who's there?
Aubrey.
  Aubrey who?
Aubrey Quiet!

Knock-knock.
  Who's there?
Auerbach.
  Auerbach who?
Please scratch
Auerbach.

Knock-knock.
  Who's there?
Auletta.
  Auletta who?
Auletta bygones be bygones!

Knock-knock.
  Who's there?
Auntie.
  Auntie who?
Auntie Aircraft!

Knock-knock.
  Who's there?
Avalon.
  Avalon who?
Avalon way to go!

Knock-knock.
  Who's there?
Avenue.
  Avenue who?
Avenue any pity?

Knock-knock.
  Who's there?
Ayatollah.
  Ayatollah who?
Ayatollah you to keep
your hands to yourself!

B

Knock-knock.
  Who's there?
Babbit.
  Babbit who?
Babbit and Costello!

Knock-knock.
  Who's there?
Bach.
  Bach who?
Bach to the future!

Knock-knock.
  Who's there?
Baldoni.
  Baldoni who?
Baldoni a
little on
the top.

Knock-knock.
  Who's there?
Barbara.
  Barbara who?
The Barbara Seville.

Knock-knock.
　Who's there?
Bea.
　Bea who?
Bea Faroni!

Knock-knock.
　Who's there?
Bee Hive.
　Bee Hive who?
Bee Hive yourself!

Knock-knock.
　Who's there?
Betty.
　Betty who?
Betty B. Careful!

Knock-knock.
　Who's there?
Blake.
　Blake who?
Blake a leg!

Knock-knock.
　Who's there?
Brigham.
　Brigham who?
Brigham a present!

Knock-knock.
　Who's there?
Bruno.
　Bruno who?
Bruno who it is!

Knock-knock.
　Who's there?
Buck and Ham.
　Buck and Ham who?
Buck and Ham Palace!

Knock-knock.
　Who's there?
Butcher.
　Butcher who?
"Butcher head on my shoulder . . ."

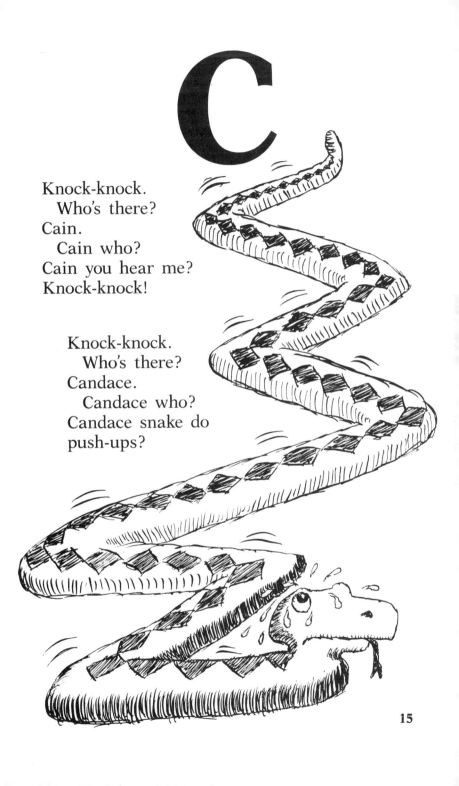

C

Knock-knock.
Who's there?
Cain.
Cain who?
Cain you hear me?
Knock-knock!

Knock-knock.
Who's there?
Candace.
Candace who?
Candace snake do
push-ups?

15

Knock-knock.
 Who's there?
Cannibal.
 Cannibal who?
Cannibal (can a bull) ice skate?

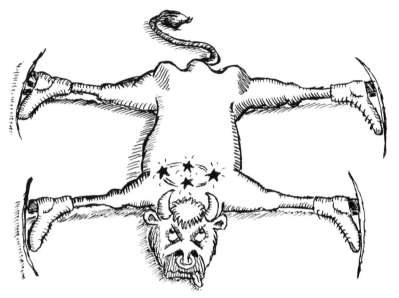

Knock-knock.
 Who's there?
Cantaloupe.
 Cantaloupe who?
Cantaloupe today, maybe tomorrow . . .

Knock-knock.
 Who's there?
Cantillo.
 Cantillo who?
Cantillo my name,
but my face will be familiar.

Knock-knock.
  Who's there?
Carmen.
  Carmen who?
" 'Carmen to my parlor,'
said the spider to the fly!"

Knock-knock.
  Who's there?
Carrie.
  Carrie who?
Carrie R. pigeon.

Knock-knock.
  Who's there?
Casanova.
  Casanova who?
Casanova (isn't over)
until the fat lady sings.

Knock-knock.
  Who's there?
Cashew.
  Cashew who?
Cashew see I'm busy?

Knock-knock.
  Who's there?
Cass.
  Cass who?
Cass Toff, we're leaving!

Knock-knock.
  Who's there?
Cassie.
  Cassie who?
Cassie Nova! How can you resist me?

  Knock-knock.
    Who's there?
  Will F.
    Will F. who?
  Will F. Iron.

Knock-knock.
  Who's there?
Cassie.
  Cassie who?
Cassie O. Watch!

Knock-knock.
  Who's there?
Cassie.
  Cassie who?
Cassie you now—
I've got to run!

Knock-knock.
  Who's there?
Cassius.
  Cassius who?
Cassius if you can!

  Knock-knock.
    Who's there?
  Cattle Drive.
    Cattle Drive who?
  This Cattle (cat will) Drive you crazy!

Knock-knock.
  Who's there?
Celeste.
  Celeste who?
Celeste you know the better!

Knock-knock.
  Who's there?
Cher.
  Cher who?
Cher would be nice if you opened the door!

Knock-knock.
  Who's there?
Cherry.
  Cherry who?
Cherry Lewis!

Knock-knock.
  Who's there?
Chester.
  Chester who?
Chester little kid!

Knock-knock.
  Who's there?
Chicken.
  Chicken who?
Just Chicken
out the
doorbell!

Knock-knock.
  Who's there?
Coed.
  Coed who?
Coed (go ahead),
make my day!!

Knock-knock.
  Who's there?
Cohen.
  Cohen who?
Cohen home—goodbye!

Knock-knock.
  Who's there?
Cummings.
  Cummings who?
Cummings back tomorrow!

Knock-knock.
  Who's there?
Coincidental.
  Coincidental who?
Coincidental (go in the dental) chair
and have your teeth cleaned.

Knock-knock.
  Who's there?
Count Aaron.
  Count Aaron who?
Count Aaron-telligence.

Knock-knock.
  Who's there?
Crassus.
  Crassus who?
Crassus always greener on the other side!

Knock-knock.
  Who's there?
Culligan.
  Culligan who?
I'll Culligan when you have
something intelligent to say.

Knock-knock.
  Who's there?
Culver.
  Culver who?
Culver me up, I'm freezing.

Knock-knock.
  Who's there?
Czar.
  Czar who?
Czar-y about that!

Knock-knock.
  Who's there?
Apollo.
  Apollo who?
Apollo G. Accepted!

D

Knock-knock.
  Who's there?
Dakar.
  Dakar who?
Dakar has a flat tire!

Knock-knock.
  Who's there?
Dakota.
  Dakota who?
Dakota many colors.

Knock-knock.
  Who's there?
Damascus.
  Damascus who?
Damascus slipping
off da face.

Knock-knock.
  Who's there?
Dancer.
  Dancer who?
"Dancer, my friend, is blowing in the wind . . ."

Knock-knock.
  Who's there?
Daniella.
  Daniella who?
Daniella (don't yell at) me, I can hear you!

22

Knock-knock.
  Who's there?
Darren.
    Darren who?
Darren you to open the door!

    Knock-knock.
      Who's there?
    New Year.
        New Year who?
    New Year (knew you were)
    going to say that!

Knock-knock.
  Who's there?
Deanne.
    Deanne who?
I'm Deanne-sir to your prayers!

    Knock-knock.
      Who's there?
    Gallo.
        Gallo who?
    Gallo your dreams

Knock-knock.
  Who's there?
Morgan.
    Morgan who?
Morgan just a pretty face!

Knock-knock.
  Who's there?
Dee Wallace.
  Dee Wallace who?
"Dee Wallace came tumbling down!"

  Knock-knock.
    Who's there?
  Eye Sore.
    Eye Sore who?
  Eye Sore them coming!

Knock-knock.
  Who's there?
Diane Kilburn.
  Diane Kilburn who?
"Diane Kilburn's (the ankle bone's)
connected to the foot bone..."

    Knock-knock.
      Who's there?
    Dog Catcher.
      Dog Catcher who?
    Dog Catcher (don't count your)
    chickens before they hatch!

Knock-knock.
  Who's there?
Donald.
  Donald who?
Donald (don't hold) your breath!

Knock-knock.
  Who's there?
Don Blaine.
  Don Blaine who?
Don Blaine (don't blame) me!

Knock-knock.
  Who's there?
Don Boris Witty.
  Don Boris Witty who?
Don Boris Witty details!

Knock-knock.
  Who's there?
Don Marcus.
  Don Marcus who?
Don Marcus absent, we're right here!

Knock-knock.
  Who's there?
Donovan.
  Donovan who?
Donovan think about it!

Knock-knock.
  Who's there?
Dona Lewis.
  Dona Lewis who?
Dona Lewis (don't lose) your temper!

Knock-knock.
  Who's there?
Donna.
  Donna who?
"Way Donna-pon the Swanee River . . ."

Knock-knock.
  Who's there?
Doris.
  Doris who?
Doris no fool like an old fool!

Knock-knock.
　Who's there?
Dozer.
　Dozer who?
Dozer the breaks!

Knock-knock.
　Who's there?
Dragon.
　Dragon who?
Quit Dragon your
tail!

　Knock-knock.
　　Who's there?
　Autumn.
　　Autumn who?
　You Autumn mind
　your own business!

Knock-knock.
　Who's there?
Dudes.
　Dudes who?
Dudes and don'ts.

Knock-knock.
　Who's there?
Duncan.
　Duncan who?
Duncan Donuts.

Knock-knock.
  Who's there?
Druscilla.
  Druscilla who?
Druscilla (drew a silly)
picture of the teacher.

  Knock-knock.
    Who's there?
  Mamie.
    Mamie who?
  She Mamie erase it.

Knock-knock.
  Who's there?
Dwayne.
  Dwayne who?
"Dwayne in Spain falls
mainly in the plain . . ."

  Knock-knock.
    Who's there?
  Wayne.
    Wayne who?
  "Wayne, Wayne, go away,
  come again another day!"

E

Knock-knock.
  Who's there?
Eiffel Tower.
  Eiffel Tower who?
Eiffel (I feel) Towerble!

  Knock-knock.
    Who's there?
  Elaine.
    Elaine who?
  Elaine down
  to take a nap.

  Knock-knock.
    Who's there?
  Ma Belle.
    Ma Belle who?
  Ma Belle E. aches.

    Knock-knock.
      Who's there?
    Cara Mia.
      Cara Mia who?
    Cara Mia to the doctor!

Knock-knock.
  Who's there?
Emma Lou King.
  Emma Lou King who?
Emma Lou King into my crystal ball . . .

Knock-knock.
  Who's there?
Emma.
  Emma who?
Emma Nemms!

Knock-knock.
  Who's there?
Encino.
  Encino who?
Hear no evil, speak
no evil, Encino evil!

Knock-knock.
  Who's there?
Enid Sue.
  Enid Sue who?
Enid Sue like a
hole in the head!

Knock-knock.
  Who's there?
Errol.
  Errol who?
Errol be a hot time in the old town tonight!

Knock-knock.
  Who's there?
Estelle.
  Estelle who?
Estelle am waiting for you to open this door!

Knock-knock.
  Who's there?
Etta May Whit.
  Etta May Whit who?
Etta May Whit- (At my wits') send!

Knock-knock.   Knock-knock.
  Who's there?   Who's there?
Etta.   Eubie.
  Etta who?   Eubie who?
Etta Boy!   "Eubie long to me . . ."

Knock-knock.
  Who's there?
Eudora Belle.
  Eudora Belle who?
Eudora Belle thing, you!

    Knock-knock.
      Who's there?
    Goddess.
      Goddess who?
    Goddess stop meeting like this.

Knock-knock.
  Who's there?
Eudora.
  Eudora who?
Eudora is stuck!

Knock-knock.
  Who's there?
Europe.
  Europe who?
Europe (you're up)
to no good!

Knock-knock.
  Who's there?
Evan.
  Evan who?
Evan Lee coffee!

Knock-knock.
  Who's there?
Ewell.
  Ewell who?
Ewell catch more flies
with honey than with vinegar!

F

Knock-knock.
　Who's there?
Fallacy.
　Fallacy who?
I Fallacy (fail to see)
what's so funny!

Knock-knock.
　Who's there?
Fanny.
　Fanny who?
Fanny you should ask!

Knock-knock.
　Who's there?
Far Side.
　Far Side who?
As Far Side (far as I) know, it's still me!

Knock-knock.
　Who's there?
Farrah.
　Farrah who?
Farrah 'n wide.

Knock-knock.
　Who's there?
Father.
　Father who?
The Father the better!

33

Knock-knock.
  Who's there?
Fatso Kay.
  Fatso Kay who?
Fatso Kay with you, Fatso Kay with me!

Knock-knock.
  Who's there?
Ferrara.
  Ferrara who?
"Long ago and Ferrara-way . . ."

Knock-knock.
  Who's there?
Fiendish.
  Fiendish who?
Fiendish your dinner!

Knock-knock.
  Who's there?
Fission.
  Fission who?
Fission for compliments!

Knock-knock.
  Who's there?
Fitzhugh.
  Fitzhugh who?
If the shoe Fitzhugh wear it!

Knock-knock.
  Who's there?
Flaherty.
  Flaherty who?
Flaherty will get you nowhere!

Knock-knock.
  Who's there?
Florist.
  Florist who?
You can't see the
Florist for the trees!

Knock-knock.
  Who's there?
Fonzi.
  Fonzi who?
Fonzi meeting you here!

Knock-knock.
  Who's there?
Ford.
  Ford who?
Ford-y thieves.

Knock-knock.
  Who's there?
Foreign.
  Foreign who?
"Foreign twenty blackbirds baked in a pie . . ."

35

Knock-knock.
Who's there?
Formosa.
Formosa who?
Formosa my life, I've been waiting for you to open the door!

Knock-knock.
Who's there?
Fred.
Fred who?
Fred I'll have to tell
you another joke. . . .

Knock-knock.
Who's there?
Freeze.
Freeze who?
"Freeze a jolly good fellow . . ."

Knock-knock.
Who's there?
Frieda.
Frieda who?
Who's a Frieda the big bad wolf?

Knock-knock.
Who's there?
Doughnut.
Doughnut who?
Doughnut be afraid—it's only me!

G

Knock-knock.
  Who's there?
G-Man.
  G-Man who?
G-Man-y Crickets!

Knock-knock.
  Who's there?
Galahad.
  Galahad who?
I knew a Galahad
two left feet!

Knock-knock.
  Who's there?
Garcia.
  Garcia who?
Garcia (go see) the principal.

Knock-knock.
  Who's there?
Garter.
  Garter who?
Garter go now!

Knock-knock.
  Who's there?
Gauguin.
  Gauguin who?
Gauguin, it's your turn!

Knock-knock.
  Who's there?
Gavin.
  Gavin who?
Gavin you one more chance
to open the door!

    Knock-knock.
      Who's there?
    Dustin.
      Dustin who?
    Dustin off the battering ram!

        Knock-knock.
          Who's there?
        Germaine.
          Germaine who?
        Germaine (you're mean)
        to act this way!

Knock-knock.
  Who's there?
Gibbon.
  Gibbon who?
Are you Gibbon me trouble?

    Knock-knock.
      Who's there?
    Gil Diaz.
      Gil Diaz who?
    Gil Diaz (guilty as) charged!

Knock-knock.
  Who's there?
GM.
  GM who?
GM I rattling your cage?

Knock-knock.
  Who's there?
Goddard.
  Goddard who?
You Goddard be kidding!

Knock-knock.
  Who's there?
Aikido.
  Aikido who?
Aikido you not!

Knock-knock.
  Who's there?
Goody.
  Goody who?
"Goody-vening!" says Count Dracula.

    Knock-knock.
      Who's there?
    Venom.
      Venom who?
    Venom I going to get inside?

        Knock-knock.
          Who's there?
        Vicious.
          Vicious who?
        Best Vicious!

Knock-knock.
  Who's there?
Gray Z.
  Gray Z. who?
Gray Z. mixed-up kid!

Knock-knock.
  Who's there?
Guava.
  Guava who?
Guava good time!

Knock-knock.
  Who's there?
Guinesss.
  Guinness who?
Guinness a break!

Knock-knock.
  Who's there?
Giuseppe.
  Giuseppe who?
Giuseppe (just stepped) in
something on your doorstep.

  Knock-knock.
    Who's there?
  Houdini.
    Houdini who?
  Houdini that thing on your doorstep?

Knock-knock.
  Who's there?
Gummy.
  Gummy who?
Gummy five!

Knock-knock.
  Who's there?
Gwynn N.
  Gwynn N. who?
Gwynn N. bear it!

H

Knock-knock.
Who's there?
Habit.
Habit who?
Habit your own way!

Knock-knock.
Who's there?
Hair Combs.
Hair Combs who?
Hair Combs the Judge!

Knock-knock.
  Who's there?
Harrison.
  Harrison who?
Harrison idea—you tell the next joke!

Knock-knock.
  Who's there?
Hartley.
  Hartley who?
This is Hartley the time
to be telling knock-knock jokes!

Knock-knock.
  Who's there?
Ed Rather.
  Ed Rather who?
Ed Rather be sailing!

Knock-knock.
  Who's there?
Harv and Hugh.
  Harv and Hugh who?
Harv and Hugh (haven't you) got a minute?

Knock-knock.
  Who's there?
Hedda.
  Hedda who?
Hedda I win, tails you lose!

Knock-knock.
  Who's there?
Healy.
  Healy who?
Healy my pain . . .

Knock-knock.
  Who's there?
Heidi.
  Heidi who?
Heidi go seek.

Knock-knock.
  Who's there?
Hello Etta.
  Hello Etta who?
"Hello Etta, gentille Alouetta . . ."

Knock-knock.
  Who's there?
Hiram.
  Hiram who?
Hiram glad you asked!

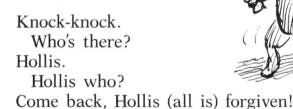

Knock-knock.
  Who's there?
Hollis.
  Hollis who?
Come back, Hollis (all is) forgiven!

          Knock-knock.
            Who's there?
          Honda.
            Honda who?
          Honda road again!

Knock-knock.
 Who's there?
Honorless.
 Honorless who?
Honorless you open this door,
I'll have to break it down!

Knock-knock.
 Who's there?
Hoodoo.
 Hoodoo who?
Hoodoo you want it to be?

   Knock-knock.
    Who's there?
   San Juan.
    San Juan who?
   San Juan (someone) else!

   Knock-knock.
    Who's there?
   Asta.
    Asta who?
   Asta La Veesta, baby!

Knock-knock.
 Who's there?
Horace.
 Horace who?
Horace of a different color!

Knock-knock.
 Who's there?
House.
 House who?
House it going?

Knock-knock.
 Who's there?
Howard.
 Howard who?
Howard you like to crawl
back under your rock?

Knock-knock.
 Who's there?
Hubie Maddern.
 Hubie Maddern who?
Hubie Maddern
a wet hen!

Knock-knock.
 Who's there?
Hugo N.
 Hugo N. who?
Hugo N. Crazy—
and I'm goin' home.

Knock-knock.
 Who's there?
Hyam Alda.
 Hyam Alda who?
Hyam Alda washed up!

I

Knock-knock.
  Who's there?
Ice Water.
  Ice Water who?
My Ice Water
when I chop onions!

Knock-knock.
  Who's there?
Icon.
  Icon who?
Icon live without you!

Knock-knock.
  Who's there?
Ida Clair.
  Ida Clair who?
Ida Clair, you're the
most stubborn person!

Knock-knock.
  Who's there?
Ida Klein.
  Ida Klein who?
Ida Klein to answer
that question!

Knock-knock.
　Who's there?
Iodine.
　Iodine who?
Iodine (I'm a dyin') for a pizza!

Knock-knock.
　Who's there?
Iris.
　Iris who?
Iris I could rock you to sleep—
with big ones!

Knock-knock.
　Who's there?
Cotton.
　Cotton who?
Cotton off to a bad start!

Knock-knock.
　Who's there?
Combat.
　Combat who?
Combat tomorrow!

Knock-knock.
　Who's there?
Isabelle.
　Isabelle who?
Isabelle broken?

Knock-knock.
　Who's there?
Isadore.
　Isadore who?
Isadore stuck?

Knock-knock.
  Who's there?
Isaiah.
  Isaiah who?
Isaiah there, old chap,
why don't you open the door?

Knock-knock.
  Who's there?
Istanbul.
  Istanbul who?
Istanbul fight over?

Knock-knock.
  Who's there?
Ivan.
  Ivan who?
"Ivan working on the railroad..."

J

Knock-knock.
 Who's there?
Jack N.
 Jack N. who?
Jack N. the Box.

Knock-knock.
 Who's there?
Jackel.
 Jackel who?
Jackel lantern.

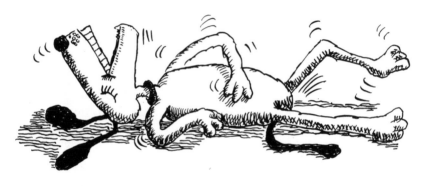

Knock-knock.
 Who's there?
Janet R.
 Janet R. who?
Janet R. in a drum.

Knock-knock.
 Who's there?
Jeff.
 Jeff who?
Jeff Boy-R-Dee.

Knock-knock.
 Who's there?
Jericho.
 Jericho who?
Jericho to Disneyland?

Knock-knock.
 Who's there?
Jerome.
 Jerome who?
Have it Jerome way!

Knock-knock.
 Who's there?
Jess B.
 Jess B. who?
Jess B. Cuzz!

Knock-knock.
 Who's there?
Jess Horace.
 Jess Horace who?
Jess Horace-n' around!

Knock-knock.
 Who's there?
Jester.
 Jester who?
Jester minute, I've got more
knock-knock jokes!

Knock-knock.
 Who's there?
Jethro.
 Jethro who?
Jethro (just throw)
me a few bones.

Knock-knock.
 Who's there?
Jock.
 Jock who?
Jock-late milk shake.

Knock-knock.
 Who's there?
Juan.
 Juan who?
Juan good turn deserves another!

Knock-knock.
  Who's there?
Juan.
  Juan who?
Juan two, buckle my shoe . . .

  Knock-knock.
    Who's there?
  Grigor.
    Grigor who?
  Grigor (three, four), shut the door . . .

Knock-knock.
  Who's there?
Physics.
  Physics who?
Physics (five, six), pick up sticks.

  Knock-knock.
    Who's there?
  Stefan Haight.
    Stefan Haight who?
  Stefan Haight, lay them straight.

Knock-knock.
  Who's there?
Jubilee.
  Jubilee who?
Jubilee-ve in the tooth fairy?

K

Knock-knock.
  Who's there?
Kareem Cohen.
  Kareem Cohen who?
Ice Kareem Cohen!

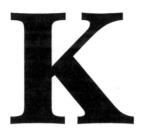

Knock-knock.
  Who's there?
Karen.
  Karen who?
Karen-teed to crack you up!

Knock-knock.
  Who's there?
Keith.
  Keith who?
Keith me, you fool!

Knock-knock.
  Who's there?
Ken D.
  Ken D. who?
Ken D. gram.

Knock-knock.
  Who's there?
Kiefer.
  Kiefer who?
Kiefer stiff upper lip.

Knock-knock.
  Who's there?
Kenya.
  Kenya who?
Kenya hear me knocking?
I said "Knock-knock!"

Knock-knock.
  Who's there?
Kevin.
  Kevin who?
"Thank Kevin
for little girls . . ."

Knock-knock.
  Who's there?
Klaus.
  Klaus who?
Klaus your mouth and open the door!

Knock-knock.
  Who's there?
Koala.
  Koala who?
Koala-T jokes like these are hard to find.

Knock-knock.   Knock-knock.
  Who's there?   Who's there?
Kris.   Kurt.
  Kris who?   Kurt who?
Kris P. Critters!   Kurt that out!

54

L

Knock-knock.
  Who's there?
L.B.
  L.B. who?
L.B. the judge of that!

Knock-knock.
  Who's there?
Leah Penn.
  Leah Penn who?
Leah Penn Lizards!

Knock-knock.
  Who's there?
Lettuce.
  Lettuce who?
Lettuce discuss this like mature adults . . .

Knock-knock.
 Who's there?
Linda.
 Linda who?
Linda helping hand.

 Knock-knock.
  Who's there?
 Yukon.
  Yukon who?
 Yukon count on me.

Knock-knock.
 Who's there?
Lionel.
 Lionel who?
Lionel get you in trouble!

Knock-knock.
 Who's there?
Lucy.
 Lucy who?
Lucy Nupp!

Knock-knock.
 Who's there?
Luke.
 Luke who?
Luke out below!

 Knock-knock.
  Who's there?
 Lyndon.
  Lyndon who?
 Lyndon Ear!

M

Knock-knock.
Who's there?
Mabel.
Mabel who?
Mabel I'll tell you and Mabel I won't!

Knock-knock.
Who's there?
Mack.
Mack who?
Mack up your mind!

Knock-knock.
Who's there?
Madge.
Madge who?
Madge N. that!

Knock-knock.
Who's there?
Ma Harrison.
Ma Harrison who?
Ma Harrison (my hair is on) fire!

Knock-knock.
Who's there?
Mannheim.
Mannheim who?
Mannheim tired!

Knock-knock.
  Who's there?
Manny Dunn.
  Manny Dunn who?
Manny Dunn
grow on trees.

Knock-knock.
  Who's there?
Mansion.
  Mansion who?
Did I Mansion I have
more knock-knock jokes?

Knock-knock.
  Who's there?
Marsha.
  Marsha who?
Marsha Mallow!

Knock-knock.
  Who's there?
Math.
  Math who?
Math (mashed) Potatoes!

Knock-knock.
  Who's there?
May Kay.
  May Kay who?
May Kay while the sun shines!

Knock-knock.
  Who's there?
Mazda.
  Mazda who?
Mazda of the Universe!

Knock-knock.
  Who's there?
Midas.
  Midas who?
Midas well try again—knock-knock!

    Knock-knock.
      Who's there?
    Mike Rowe.
      Mike Rowe who?
    Mike Rowe wave oven.

Knock-knock.
  Who's there?
Missouri.
  Missouri who?
Missouri (misery) loves company!

  Knock-knock.
    Who's there?
  William.
    William who?
  William miss me when I'm gone?

    Knock-knock.
      Who's there?
    Mischief.
      Mischief who?
    I guess I'd Mischief (miss you if)
    you left . . .

N

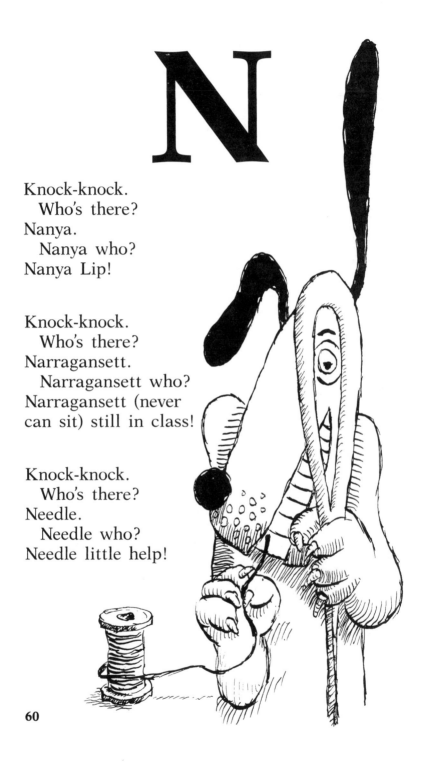

Knock-knock.
  Who's there?
Nanya.
  Nanya who?
Nanya Lip!

Knock-knock.
  Who's there?
Narragansett.
  Narragansett who?
Narragansett (never
can sit) still in class!

Knock-knock.
  Who's there?
Needle.
  Needle who?
Needle little help!

Knock-knock.
  Who's there?
Nefertiti.
  Nefertiti who?
Nefertiti (never teeter) totter
with a 500-pound gorilla!!

Knock-knock.
  Who's there?
Albee.
  Albee who?
Albee a monkey's uncle!

Knock-knock.
  Who's there?
Nemo.
  Nemo who?
Nemo time to think
of a joke!

Knock-knock.
  Who's there?
Noah.
  Noah who?
There's Noah-scape!

Knock-knock.
  Who's there?
Nevada.
  Nevada who?
You Nevada had it so good!

　　Knock-knock.
　　 Who's there?
　　Gouda.
　　 Gouda who?
　　This is as Goudas it gets!

　　　　Knock-knock.
　　　　 Who's there?
　　　　Osgood.
　　　　 Osgood who?
　　　　Osgood S. Canby.

Knock-knock.
  Who's there?
Nora Marx.
  Nora Marx who?
Nora Marx (no remarks)
from the peanut gallery!

　　Knock-knock.
　　 Who's there?
　　Avery.
　　 Avery who?
　　Avery body's gettin' into the act!

O

Knock-knock.
  Who's there?
O'Casey.
  O'Casey who?
O'Casey if I care!

Knock-knock.
  Who's there?
O'Keefe.
  O'Keefe who?
"O'Keefe me a
home where the
buffalo roam . . ."

Knock-knock.
  Who's there?
Obi Wan.
  Obi Wan who?
Obi Wan-derful and
take me to the movies!

Knock-knock.
  Who's there?
Odaris.
  Odaris who?
Odaris a bee on
your shoulder!

Knock-knock.
  Who's there?
Odd Thing.
  Odd Thing who?
Odd Thing (I'd sing)
all day if I knew a thong!

        Knock-knock.
          Who's there?
        Odyssey.
          Odyssey who?
        Odyssey (hard to see) how you made
        it past the first grade!

Knock-knock.
  Who's there?
Offer.
  Offer who?
Offer Got (I forgot)!

Knock-knock.
  Who's there?
Oink.
  Oink who?
Oink L. Sam!

Knock-knock.
  Who's there?
Olivia.
  Olivia who?
Olivia lone if that's
what you want!

Knock-knock.
  Who's there?
Nevil.
  Nevil who?
Nevil mind!

Knock-knock.
  Who's there?
Otto.
  Otto who?
Your bell is
Otto order.

Knock-knock.
  Who's there?
Owen Williams.
  Owen Williams who?
Owen Williams (oh, when
will you) open this door?

P

Knock-knock.
  Who's there?
Panda.
  Panda who?
Panda monium!

Knock-knock.
  Who's there?
Pasta.
  Pasta who?
Pasta pizza under the door—I'm starved!

Knock-knock.
  Who's there?
Azenauer.
  Azenauer who?
Azenauer (has an hour) gone by
since you put the pizza in the oven?

Knock-knock.
 Who's there?
Pasteur.
 Pasteur who?
It's Pasteur (past your) bedtime!

Knock-knock.
 Who's there?
Patton.
 Patton who?
Patton leather shoes!

Knock-knock.
 Who's there?
Paul.
 Paul who?
Paul-tergeist!

Knock-knock.
 Who's there?
Peapod.
 Peapod who?
I don't want to hear a
Peapod (peep out of) you!

Knock-knock.
 Who's there?
Percy.
 Percy who?
Percy-veere (persevere)!

Knock-knock.
 Who's there?
Phyllis.
 Phyllis who?
Phyllis in on the details!

Knock-knock.
  Who's there?
Pinafore.
  Pinafore who?
Pinafore for your thoughts . . .

Knock-knock.
  Who's there?
Pitcher.
  Pitcher who?
Pitcher money where your mouth is!

Knock-knock.
  Who's there?
Pizza.
  Pizza who?
Pizza nice guy when you get to know him.

Knock-knock.
  Who's there?
Police.
  Police who?
Police B. Careful!

Knock-knock.
  Who's there?
Police.
  Police who?
Police open the door!

Knock-knock.
  Who's there?
Polly N.
  Polly N. who?
Polly N. saturated.

Knock-knock.
 Who's there?
Porsche.
 Porsche who?
Porsche me in the right direction!

Knock-knock.
 Who's there?
Pudding.
 Pudding who?
Pudding my best foot forward!

Knock-knock.
 Who's there?
Pumpkin.
 Pumpkin who?
A thing that goes pumpkin
(bump in) the night.

Knock-knock.
 Who's there?
Pyrite.
 Pyrite who?
Pyrite in your face—Pow!

Knock-knock.
  Who's there?
Quibble.
  Quibble who?
Quibble and Bits.

Knock-knock.
  Who's there?
Quigley.
  Quigley who?
Open the door Quigley, I must get in!

Knock-knock.
  Who's there?
Wilson.
  Wilson who?
Wilson body let me in?

R

Knock-knock.
 Who's there?
Raisin.
 Raisin who?
Raisin Cane!

Knock-knock.
 Who's there?
Rajah.
 Rajah who?
Rajah Rabbit!

Knock-knock.
 Who's there?
Rambo.
 Rambo who?
"Somewhere, over the Rambo . . ."

Knock-knock.
 Who's there?
Ray and Greta.
 Ray and Greta who?
You'll Ray Greta asking me that!

Knock-knock.
 Who's there?
Renata.
 Renata who?
Renata (run out of) steam?

Knock-knock.
　Who's there?
Rhett.
　Rhett who?
Rhett-urn of the Jedi.

Knock-knock.
　Who's there?
Rick.
　Rick who?
Rick Shaw,
hop in for a ride!

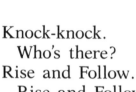

Knock-knock.
　Who's there?
Rise and Follow.
　Rise and Follow who?
Rise and Follow (rise and fall of)
the Roman Empire.

Knock-knock.
　Who's there?
Rita.
　Rita who?
Rita my lips!

Knock-knock.
　Who's there?
Robert de Niro.
　Robert de Niro who?
Robert de Niro, but he's not here yet.

Knock-knock.
  Who's there?
Robert Redford.
  Robert Redford who?
Robert Redford the part in the play.

    Knock-knock.
      Who's there?
    Romanoff.
      Romanoff who?
    There ain't Romanoff for the
    both of us in this town!

Knock-knock.   Knock-knock.
  Who's there?   Who's there?
Ron.   Ronan.
  Ron who?   Ronan who?
Ron for your life!   Ronan amuck!

Knock-knock.   Knock-knock.
  Who's there?   Who's there?
Roy.   Russ.
  Roy who?   Russ who?
Roy L. Flush!   Russ Crispies!

Knock-knock.
 Who's there?
Safaris.
  Safaris who?
Safaris I can see, it's me!

Knock-knock.
 Who's there?
Santucci.
  Santucci who?
Santucci my sunburn!

Knock-knock.
 Who's there?
Santa.
  Santa who?
Santa Mental Fool!

Knock-knock.
 Who's there?
Sasha.
  Sasha who?
Sasha dummy!

Knock-knock.
 Who's there?
Saul and Terry.
  Saul and Terry who?
Saul and Terry confinement!

Knock-knock.
 Who's there?
Saul Upp.
  Saul Upp who?
Saul Upp to you!

Knock-knock.
 Who's there?
Schenectady.
 Schenectady who?
Schenectady (the neck of the) shirt is
too tight.

Knock-knock.
 Who's there?
Scoot.
 Scoot who?
Scoot to be here!

Knock-knock.
 Who's there?
Scott.
 Scott who?
Scott to be me!

Knock-knock.
 Who's there?
Sea Bass.
 Sea Bass who?
Sea Bass-tian the crab.

Knock-knock.
 Who's there?
Shafter.
 Shafter who?
Shafter make a phone call!

Knock-knock.
 Who's there?
Shelby and Carmen.
 Shelby and Carmen who?
"Shelby Carmen round the mountain
when she comes!"

Knock-knock.
  Who's there?
Shelley.
  Shelley who?
Shelley try again?

  Knock-knock.
    Who's there?
  Dozen.
    Dozen who?
  Dozen matter to me!

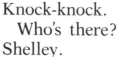

Knock-knock.
  Who's there?
Shopper Dan.
  Shopper Dan who?
You're Shopper Dan
(sharpen than) I thought!

Knock-knock.
  Who's there?
Sloan.
  Sloan who?
Sloan (slow and) steady wins the race!

Knock-knock.
  Who's there?
Sly Dover.
  Sly Dover who?
Sly Dover, I'm breaking down the door!

Knock-knock.
  Who's there?
Sodium.
  Sodium who?
Sodium (so do you) mind if I come in?

Knock-knock.
  Who's there?
Sonny N.
  Sonny N. who?
Sonny N. clear today—rain tomorrow!

  Knock-knock.
    Who's there?
  Wanda.
    Wanda who?
  Wanda come out and play?

Knock-knock.
  Who's there?
Sony.
  Sony who?
Sony your old pal . . .

  Knock-knock.
    Who's there?
  Trotter.
    Trotter who?
  Trotter remember me.

Knock-knock.
  Who's there?
Spetzel.
  Spetzel who?
Spetzel delivery!!

Knock-knock.
  Who's there?
Spook.
  Spook who?
I Spook too soon!

Knock-knock.
  Who's there?
Stan and Bea.
  Stan and Bea who?
Stan Dupp and
Bea Counted!

Knock-knock.
  Who's there?
Surreal.
  Surreal who?
Surreal pleasure to be here!

Knock-knock.
  Who's there?
Sven.
  Sven who?
Sven are you going to open the door?

T

Knock-knock.
  Who's there?
Tamara.
  Tamara who?
Tamara Boom-dee-ay!

Knock-knock.
  Who's there?
Tennessee.
  Tennessee who?
Is that a Tennessee (tan I see),
or haven't you bathed lately?

Knock-knock.
  Who's there?
Tess Slater.
  Tess Slater who?
Tess Slater than
you think!

Knock-knock.
  Who's there?
The Genius.
  The Genius who?
The Genius (the genie is) out of the bottle.

Knock-knock.
  Who's there?
The Ghost.
  The Ghost who?
The Ghost is clear—let's go!

Knock-knock.
  Who's there?
Threadbare.
  Threadbare who?
Threadbare-n (the Red Baron)
and Snoopy the Flying Ace.

Knock-knock.
  Who's there?
Thud.
  Thud who?
Thud you'd never ask!

        Knock-knock.
          Who's there?
        Thurston.
          Thurston who?
        Thurston for some water!

Knock-knock.
  Who's there?
Tijuana.
  Tijuana who?
Tijuana try for two out of three?

Knock-knock.
  Who's there?
Tom Hills.
  Tom Hills who?
Tom Hills (time heals) all wounds!

Knock-knock.
  Who's there?
Tommy.
  Tommy who?
I have a Tommy Ache!

Knock-knock.
  Who's there?
Toreador.
  Toreador who?
Toreador down—
now can I come in?

Knock-knock.
  Who's there?
Top Hat.
  Top Hat who?
Top Hat (stop that)—you're bothering me!

Knock-knock.
  Who's there?
Triton.
  Triton who?
"Triton remember the
kind of September . . ."

Knock-knock.
  Who's there?
Troy.
  Troy who?
Troy again!

  Knock-knock.
    Who's there?
  Wes D.
    Wes D. who?
  Wes D. point?

Knock-knock.
  Who's there?
Truman E.
  Truman E. who?
Truman E. cooks spoil the broth!

U

Knock-knock.
　Who's there?
Udder.
　　Udder who?
Udder Lee ridiculous!

Knock-knock.
　Who's there?
Uganda.
　Uganda who?
Uganda be kidding me!

Knock-knock.
  Who's there?
Unaware.
  Unaware who?
Your Unaware has
a hole in it!

  Knock-knock.
    Who's there?
  Tom Sawyer.
    Tom Sawyer who?
  Tom Sawyer
  underwear!

Knock-knock.
  Who's there?
Esau.
  Esau who?
Esau it too.

Knock-knock.
  Who's there?
Unique.
  Unique who?
Why do Unique (you sneak)
around on tiptoe?

              Knock-knock.
                Who's there?
              Uta May.
                Uta May who?
              Going Uta May mind!

V

Knock-knock.
 Who's there?
Vacancy.
 Vacancy who?
Vacancy (we can see) right in your window!

Knock-knock.
 Who's there?
Valley.
 Valley who?
Valley intellesting!

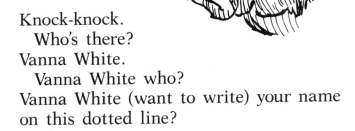

Knock-knock.
 Who's there?
Vanna White.
 Vanna White who?
Vanna White (want to write) your name
on this dotted line?

Knock-knock.
 Who's there?
Vasilli.
 Vasilli who?
Vasilli (what a silly) person you are!

Knock-knock.
  Who's there?
Vaudeville.
  Vaudeville who?
Vaudeville (what will) you be doing tonight?

Knock-knock.
  Who's there?
Vaughn.
  Vaughn who?
Vaughn to come over tomorrow?

Knock-knock.
  Who's there?
Vehicle.
  Vehicle who?
Don't call us—
Vehicle (we will call) you!

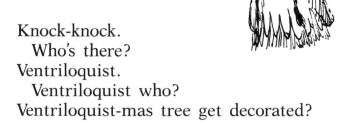

Knock-knock.
  Who's there?
Ventriloquist.
  Ventriloquist who?
Ventriloquist-mas tree get decorated?

Knock-knock.
  Who's there?
Veronica.
  Veronica who?
Veronica (we're on a c-)razy diet.

Knock-knock.
  Who's there?
Vi.
  Vi who?
Vi not?!

Knock-knock.
  Who's there?
Vile.
  Vile who?
Vile the cat's
away, the mice
vill play!

Knock-knock.
  Who's there?
Vilma.
  Vilma who?
Vilma dreams come true?

Knock-knock.
  Who's there?
Waddle.
  Waddle who?
Waddle I need to do to get you
to use your brain?

Knock-knock.
  Who's there?
Waiter.
  Waiter who?
Waiter-ound and you'll see!

Knock-knock.
  Who's there?
Walter D.
  Walter D. who?
Walter D. Lawn.

Knock-knock.
  Who's there?
Wanda.
  Wanda who?
Wanda these days—Pow!

Knock-knock.
  Who's there?
Warden.
  Warden who?
Warden the world are you up to?

Knock-knock.
  Who's there?
Warren.
  Warren who?
I'm Warren out!

Knock-knock.
  Who's there?
Warren D.
  Warren D. who?
Warren D. world are you?

Knock-knock.
  Who's there?
Wash Out.
  Wash Out who?
Wash Out, I'm coming in!

Knock-knock.
  Who's there?
Water.
  Water who?
Water friends for?

Knock-knock.
  Who's there?
Wayne.
  Wayne who?
I'm Wayne D. Outfield.

Knock-knock.
  Who's there?
Wire.
  Wire who?
Wire we telling knock-knock jokes?

    Knock-knock.
      Who's there?
    Wooden.
      Wooden who?
    Wooden you like to know!

      Knock-knock.
        Who's there?
      Wienie.
        Wienie who?
      Wienie more jokes like these!

        Knock-knock.
          Who's there?
        Archibald.
          Archibald who?
        Archibald real tears when he
        read these knock-knock jokes.

    Knock-knock.
      Who's there?
    Woody.
      Woody who?
    Woody lady of the house
    please open the door?

X

Knock-knock.
  Who's there?
X.
  X who?
X (Eggs) Benedict!

Knock-knock.
  Who's there?
Xavier.
  Xavier who?
Xavier self!

Knock-knock.
  Who's there?
Xenia.
  Xenia who?
Xenia open the door last week!

Knock-knock.
  Who's there?
Oh Mama!
  Oh Mama who?
Oh Mama-stake (oh, my mistake)!

Y

Knock-knock.
  Who's there?
Yates.
  Yates who?
Crazy Yates (Eights)!

Knock-knock.
  Who's there?
Yogurt.
  Yogurt who?
Yogurt to be joking!

Knock-knock.
  Who's there?
Arno.
  Arno who?
Arno you don't!

Knock-knock.
  Who's there?
Yokohama.
  Yokohama who?
Yokohama (you can have my) place in line!

92

Knock-knock.
  Who's there?
Yolette.
  Yolette who?
Would Yolette me in the door, please?

  Knock-knock.
    Who's there?
  Wilma.
    Wilma who?
  Wilma jokes make you open the door?

    Knock-knock.
      Who's there?
    Ozzie.
      Ozzie who?
    Ozzie (I see) I'm going to be
    out here all night.

      Knock-knock.
        Who's there?
      Yukon.
        Yukon who?
      Yukon say that again!

Knock-knock.
  Who's there?
Yukon.
  Yukon who?
Yukon (you can't) teach
an old dog new tricks!

Z

Knock-knock.
  Who's there?
Zany.
  Zany who?
Zany body out there?!

Knock-knock.
  Who's there?
Zelda.
  Zelda who?
Zelda family jewels!

Knock-knock.
  Who's there?
Zinc.
  Zinc who?
Zinc or swim!

Knock-knock.
  Who's there?
Zits.
  Zits who?
Zits down
and concentrate.

Knock-knock.
  Who's there?
Zoe.
  Zoe who?
Zoe (so we)
meet again!

Knock-knock.
  Who's there?
Zoo.
  Zoo who?
Zoo long for now!

  Knock-knock.
    Who's there?
  Cy.
    Cy who?
  Cy O'Nara (Sayonara)!

  Knock-knock.
    Who's there?
  Ollie-Lou.
    Ollie-Lou who?
  Ollie-Lou ya! You finally
  opened the door!

    Knock-knock.
      Who's there?
    Vienna.
      Vienna who?
    Zis is Vienna the book.

Index of Subjects and Hidden Names